JEFF GORDON

by Matt Scheff

NASCAR HEROES

Printed in the United States of America,
North Mankato, Minnesota
102012
012013

 THIS BOOK CONTAINS AT LEAST 10% RECYCLED MATERIALS.

Editor: Chrös McDougall
Series Designer: Becky Daum

Photo Credits: Autostock/Nigel Kinrade/AP Images, cover, title; Wade Payne/ AP Images, 4–5, 6–7; Mark Humphrey/AP Images, 7; Billings Gazette/Bob Zellar/AP Images, 8; Mike McCarn/AP Images, 9; ISC Images & Archives/ Getty Images, 10–11; Peter Cosgrove/AP Images, 12–13, 30 (top); Grant Halverson/AP Images, 14–15, 30 (center); Chris O'Meara/AP Images, 16–17, 18–19; Larry Giberson/AP Images, 18; Tom Ryder/AP Images, 20–21; Reed Saxon/AP Images, 22–23; Steve Helber/AP Images, 24; Tom Strattman/ AP Images, 25; Autostock/Matthew T. Thacker/AP Images, 26–27, 31; David Duprey/AP Images, 28; Paul Sancya/AP Images, 29, 30 (bottom)

Cataloging-in-Publication Data
Scheff, Matt.
 Jeff Gordon / Matt Scheff.
   p. cm. -- (NASCAR heroes)
Includes bibliographical references and index.
ISBN 978-1-61783-663-3
1. Gordon, Jeff, 1971- --Juvenile literature. 2. Automobile racing drivers-- United States--Biography--Juvenile literature.   I. Title.
796.72092--dc21
[B]

2012946250

CONTENTS

The green flag drops to start the 2002 Sharpie 500.

4

BUMP AND WIN

Jeff Gordon was in second place. Only one lap remained in the 2002 Sharpie 500 at Bristol Motor Speedway in Tennessee.

Gordon tried to pass leader Rusty Wallace, but Wallace kept blocking him. So Gordon drove his bumper into Wallace's car. Wallace's tires lost their grip. His car wiggled and slowed.

5

The bump-and-run is a racing move. To do it, a driver taps the rear corner of another car to make a pass. The contact causes the lead car's rear tires to lose grip with the track.

Gordon does a burnout after winning the 2002 Sharpie 500.

Gordon sped by Wallace. The checkered
flag waved. Gordon's bump-and-run had
won the race!

FAST FACT

Jeff Gordon began racing quarter midgets at age five. By age six, he had already won 35 events and set five track records.

Jeff raced sprint cars to help prepare him to drive bigger stock cars.

YOUNG RACER

Jeffrey Michael Gordon was born August 4, 1971, in Vallejo, California. He started racing at age five. Jeff wanted to race sprint cars when he was 13. However, California law prevented that for kids his age. So Jeff's family moved to Indiana.

He soon started to get national attention for his racing talent. In 1990, Jeff tried driving a stock car. He never looked back.

Jeff and his parents in 2006.

A NASCAR RIDE

Gordon drove his first race in National Association for Stock Car Auto Racing's (NASCAR's) second-level series in 1990. He had the second-fastest qualifying lap! But he crashed in the race and did not finish.

Two years later, in 1992, Gordon joined the Hendrick Motorsports team. He drove the No. 24 DuPont Chevrolet. His first NASCAR Cup Series race was that year. He finished thirty-first out of 41 drivers.

Gordon rounds the track during a 1991 second-level race.

FAST FACT

Jeff Gordon's first NASCAR Cup Series race was Richard Petty's last race. It was the only time the two NASCAR legends ever raced together.

WONDER BOY

Gordon was named Rookie of the Year in NASCAR's Cup Series in 1993. He won two races in 1994. One was the first Brickyard 400 at the famous Indianapolis Motor Speedway.

Gordon and longtime rival Dale Earnhardt Sr. in 1993

Approximately 350,000 fans showed up for the 1994 Brickyard 400. No NASCAR race had ever drawn that many fans.

FAST FACT
Dale Earnhardt Sr.
often teased Jeff
Gordon. He called
Gordon "Wonder Boy."

14

Gordon emerged as NASCAR's top driver starting in 1995. He beat Dale Earnhardt Sr. for the Cup Series championship. Gordon won 10 races in 1996. He was on top again in 1997. Gordon opened the season by winning his first Daytona 500. Then he won another Cup Series championship.

Gordon leads the field to the start at the 1996 Coca-Cola 600 in North Carolina.

THE RAINBOW WARRIORS

Gordon kept winning. But some fans booed him. They thought he was too confident. Many rooted for his rival, Dale Earnhardt Sr. Gordon's best season was 1998. He won 13 races that year, including four in a row, and earned his third Cup Series championship.

Gordon's Rainbow Warriors pit crew work on his car at the 1998 Pepsi 400 in Daytona Beach, Florida.

FAST FACT
Some fans chanted "A-B-G" during races in the late 1990s. A-B-G stood for "Anybody but Gordon!"

Gordon and the 2001 Cup Series trophy.

CHANGES

Gordon won seven races in 1999. He finished sixth in the Cup Series standings. His long-time crew chief, Ray Evernham, left the team after the season. Gordon struggled in 2000. Some fans said that he could not win without Evernham. But Gordon proved them wrong in 2001. He won six races and his fourth Cup Series title.

Gordon leads the pack at the 1999 Daytona 500.

DRIVE FOR FIVE

Gordon had earned four Cup Series titles through 2001. Fans called his quest for another title "the drive for five." The competition was improving. Gordon remained one of the top drivers after 2001, but that fifth championship proved just out of reach.

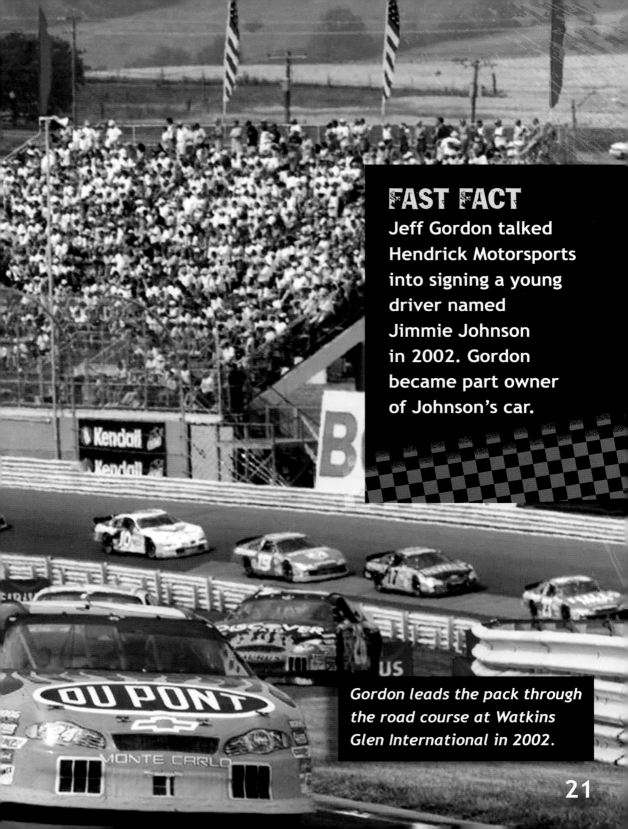

*Gordon leads the pack through
the road course at Watkins
Glen International in 2002.*

21

NASCAR changed the rules in 2004. It added a playoff system called the Chase for the Cup. It was bad timing for Gordon. He would have won the 2004 title under the old system. But he ended up third in the Chase.

Gordon's crew leads his car to Victory Lane after a 2004 win in Fontana, California.

CHASING A TEAMMATE

Gordon started the 2005 season by winning the Daytona 500. But he struggled after that. He did not make the Chase. Gordon was still one of the top drivers, but his friend and teammate Jimmie Johnson had become the best. Johnson went on to win five Sprint Cup titles between 2006 and 2010. In 2007 Gordon scored more total points than Johnson, but Johnson had a better Chase and took the Cup.

Johnson and Gordon in 2007

FAST FACT

Jeff Gordon failed to win a race in 2008. It was his first winless season since 1993.

HOLDING HIS OWN

NASCAR was changing. Talented young drivers made the competition tougher than ever. Gordon remained a solid driver, but his days of dominating the sport were gone. Gordon enjoyed a great 2011 regular season. He was near the top of the standings all year. But he did not do well in the Chase, finishing ninth.

Gordon had 85 Cup Series victories going into the 2012 season. Only two drivers had more.

LIVING LEGEND

Jeff Gordon is a legend on the track. His calm manner and great car control have made him one of the sport's all-time greats. Few drivers have dominated NASCAR the way he did in the late 1990s. He has remained one of the sport's top drivers and become a fan favorite.

Gordon has been a NASCAR star for more than two decades.

FAST FACT

Jeff Gordon lives with his wife, Ingrid, and children, Ella and Leo.

TIMELINE

1971

Jeffrey Michael Gordon is born on August 4 in Vallejo, California.

1990

Gordon drives in his first NASCAR second-level race on October 20.

1992

Gordon drives in his first Cup Series race on November 15.

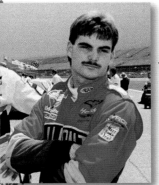

1994

Gordon wins his first Cup Series race on May 29. He also wins the first Brickyard 400.

1995

Gordon wins his first Cup Series championship.

1998

Gordon wins 13 Cup Series races and the championship.

2001

Gordon wins his fourth Cup Series championship.

2011

Gordon's victory at Atlanta moves him into third on NASCAR's all-time Cup Series wins list.

GLOSSARY

Chase
The last 10 races of the NASCAR Cup Series. Only the top 10 drivers and two wild cards qualify to race in the Chase.

Cup Series
NASCAR's top series for professional stock car drivers.

crew chief
The team member in charge of the crew and race strategy.

Daytona 500
The most famous stock car race in the world and one of the races in the Cup Series.

owner
The person who owns an entire racing team. This person hires everyone on the team, including the driver and the crew.

qualifying lap
One of two laps each driver takes before a race. The qualifying laps determine the race's starting order.

quarter midgets
Small race cars designed for short races. They are about one-fourth as large as midget cars.

rookie
A driver in his or her first full-time season in a new series.

series
A racing season that consists of several races.

sprint car
A small, open-wheel car that usually races on dirt tracks.

stock car
Race cars that resemble models of cars that people drive everyday.

INDEX